CH

UNCOVERING THE PAST:
ANALYZING PRIMARY SOURCES

LGBTQ RIGHTS

NATALIE HYDE

 Crabtree Publishing Company
www.crabtreebooks.com

Author: Natalie Hyde

Editor-in-Chief: Lionel Bender

Editors: Simon Adams, Ellen Rodger

Proofreaders: Laura Booth,
Wendy Scavuzzo

Project coordinator: Petrice Custance

Design and photo research: Ben White

Production: Kim Richardson

**Production coordinator and
prepress technician:** Ken Wright

Print coordinator: Margaret Amy Salter

Consultant: Amie Wright,
The New York Public Library

**Produced for Crabtree Publishing
Company by Bender Richardson White**

Library and Archives Canada Cataloguing in Publication

Hyde, Natalie, 1963-, author
    LGBTQ rights / Natalie Hyde.

(Uncovering the past : analyzing primary sources)
Includes bibliographical references and index.
Issued in print and electronic formats.
ISBN 978-0-7787-3942-5 (hardcover).--
ISBN 978-0-7787-3984-5 (softcover).--
ISBN 978-1-4271-2001-4 (HTML)

    1. Sexual minorities--Civil rights--History--Juvenile literature. 2. Sexual minorities--Legal status, laws, etc.-- Juvenile literature. 3. Human rights--Juvenile literature. 4. Sexual orientation--Juvenile literature. 5. Gender identity--Juvenile literature. 6. Stereotypes (Social psychology)--Juvenile literature. I. Title.

HQ73.H93 2017   j306.76   C2017-903635-1
                                        C2017-903636-X

Library of Congress Cataloging-in-Publication Data

Names: Hyde, Natalie, 1963- author.
Title: LGBTQ rights / Natalie Hyde.
Description: New York, New York : Crabtree Publishing Company, 2018.
Series: Uncovering the past : analyzing primary sources | Audience: Grades 4 to 6. | Includes bibliographical references and index.
Identifiers: LCCN 2017024374 (print) | LCCN 2017027010 (ebook) |
    ISBN 9781427120014 (Electronic HTML) |
    ISBN 9780778739425 (reinforced library binding) |
    ISBN 9780778739845 (paperback)
Subjects: LCSH: Sexual minorities--Civil rights--History--Juvenile literature. | Sexual minorities--Civil rights--History--Sources--Juvenile literature. | Sexual minorities--Legal status, laws, etc.--Juvenile literature. | Human rights--Juvenile literature. | Social movements--Juvenile literature. | Sexual orientation--Juvenile literature. | Gender identity--Juvenile literature. | Stereotypes (Social psychology)--Juvenile literature.
Classification: LCC HQ73 (ebook) | LCC HQ73 .H93 2018 (print) | DDC 306.76--dc23
LC record available at https://lccn.loc.gov/2017024374

Crabtree Publishing Company

www.crabtreebooks.com   1-800-387-7650   Printed in Canada/082017/EF20170629

Published in Canada
Crabtree Publishing
616 Welland Ave.
St. Catharines, ON
L2M 5V6

Published in the United States
Crabtree Publishing
PMB 59051
350 Fifth Avenue, 59th Floor
New York, NY 10118

Published in the United Kingdom
Crabtree Publishing
Maritime House
Basin Road North, Hove
BN41 1WR

Published in Australia
Crabtree Publishing
3 Charles Street
Coburg North
VIC, 3058

UNCOVERING THE PAST

THE PAST COMES ALIVE

"All human beings are born free and equal in dignity and rights."

United Nations (UN) Universal Declaration of Human Rights, 1948

The idea that all human beings deserve to be treated equally is a modern idea. The Universal Declaration of Human Rights by the United Nations, for example, was agreed upon only in 1948. Minorities have always had to fight for equal rights. **Immigrants,** women, disabled people, and LGBTQ (**Lesbian, Gay, Bisexual, Transgender, Queer**) have all struggled to achieve **equality** in society and in the law. The LGBTQ community has withstood **prejudice,** hatred, and fear, to claim the rights other people take for granted. Although it started in the past, LGBTQ rights is an ongoing struggle. For their symbol, the LGBTQ community has adopted the rainbow flag—its colors representing the whole **spectrum** of human genders and **sexual orientations**.

Uncovering the past is a chance for us to see how far we've come and how far we have to go. We can see past mistakes and, it is hoped, avoid them in the future. Looking back at the fight for LGBTQ rights, we can see that the struggle symbolizes a bigger fight. It is the fight for acceptance and equality under the law, no matter who you are, where you are from, your religious or cultural beliefs, or what you are dealing with. We can see that there has been some progress in aligning universal rights and civil rights for LGBTQ people. However, new governments, religious groups, and persisting prejudice in society threaten to undermine and reverse the gains that have been made.

▶ **People lining up for an event on Church Street in Toronto, Ontario, during Pride Week 2014. During Pride Week, Toronto's Gay Village closes to street traffic.**

DEFINITIONS

LGBTQ: People who are Lesbian, Gay, Bisexual, Transgender, or Queer

Human rights: Rights that are believed to belong to every person

Civil rights: The rights of citizens to political and social freedom

Equal rights: The idea that every person is to be treated equally under the law

Universal rights: Rights that are to be enjoyed by everyone

EVIDENCE RECORD CARD

People lining up for a Pride Week event

LEVEL Primary source
MATERIAL Color photograph
LOCATION Toronto, Ontario, Canada
DATE June 26, 2014
SOURCE Dreamstime photo agency

INTRODUCTION

UNCOVERING OUR PAST

Our history leaves a trail of evidence. Each time we listen to stories or read documents from the past, we gain information. When we look at paintings and photographs or listen to interviews, we are learning our history. Some evidence is stored in **archives** or museums to keep it safe. But we don't always have to go far away to find this information. Sometimes our own families or local libraries can be the place to start. With the vast reach of the Internet, we can begin to make discoveries about the past without leaving home.

Historians are people who study the past. They often specialize in one area of the world, one time period, one person, or one event. Many times, they have to be like detectives to uncover the truth about the past. Historians studying LGBTQ rights might look at first-person accounts of trials from the past, through to recent court challenges. In the past, **homosexuality** was ruled illegal and against the teachings of religious institutions. Homosexuals were afraid to let their sexual orientation be known. They knew it could lead to attacks, arrests, or even death. For the historian, this means they need to look closely to find evidence of the **abuse** of rights, as the information was often kept secret and hidden.

As the fight became more open in society, details on the first steps to equality for LGBTQ people left a bigger evidence trail. Much of it today is a legal fight, so there is a large document trail from the government and the courts. Protests and marches are public affairs that are reported on by journalists and television stations, so there is a lot of **media** coverage to examine.

"It is a tragedy, I feel, that people of a different sexual type are caught in a world which shows so little understanding for homosexuals."

American political activist and writer Emma Goldman in a letter to the German physician Magnus Hirschfeld, 1923

▼ American gay rights activist Jeff Zarrillo speaks at the California Day of Decision rally to fight for marriage equality in 2013. He later married his partner Paul Katami.

PERSPECTIVES

Words are not the only way to send a message. Look at this image of a poster from the Gay Pride events in London, England. What meaning do you see in the colors and symbols?

▼ In this poster, **Amnesty** International shows that it fights for LGBTQ individuals by shining a light on rights abuses and calling for change.

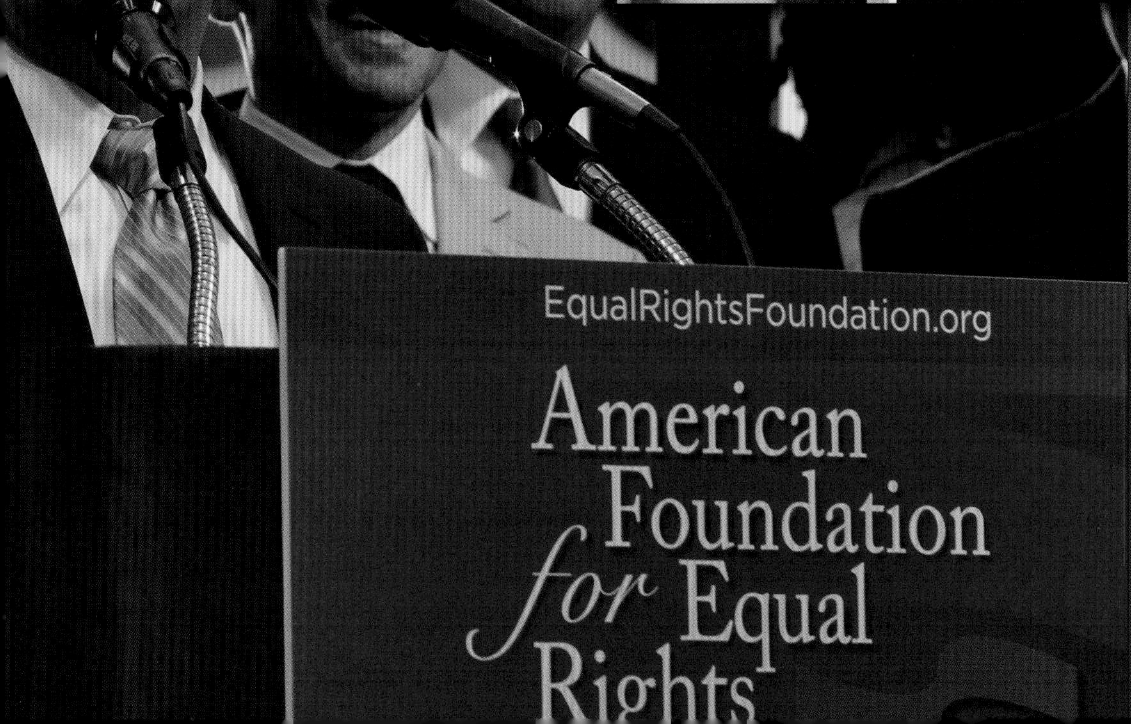

LOVE IS A HUMAN RIGHT

Amnesty International

PROTECT THE HUMAN

EqualRightsFoundation.org

American Foundation *for* Equal Rights

TYPES OF EVIDENCE

"What can be asserted without evidence can be dismissed without evidence."

Christopher Hitchens, writing in *Mommie Dearest*, Slate, October 20, 2003

Any material that remains from the past is called **source material**. Source material can be created by people involved in an event, or by people studying an event. It can be created not only by people (for example, photographs and diaries) but also by nature (fossils). It can be created on purpose (magazine article) or by accident (**body casts** of animals buried at Pompeii). Each piece of source material provides information about the person, object, or event.

Source material can be preserved in museums, archives, or personal collections. Sometimes source material is destroyed. This may happen if people want to change our understanding of the past or keep something secret. It can happen because of natural disasters such as fires or floods. Historians try to keep source material safe by keeping it in vaults, protective cases, or special rooms. Sometimes source material is preserved by chance. Old documents may be found in an attic if they were stored there, then forgotten.

Early source material about the fight for LGBTQ rights mainly consists of old court records or newspaper articles. Often these tell of homosexuals being arrested for what was once considered a criminal act. More recent source material includes gay magazines, posters from marches, and court documents. Movies and books have also explored the subject of equal rights for the LGBTQ community.

▶ Gay pride marchers in Ottawa, Canada, show their support for LGBTQ people in other parts of the world.

ANALYZE THIS

Why is it important to keep early records and articles about LGBTQ rights even if they show misunderstanding and disrespect for homosexual, transgender, or **gender-fluid** people? What can we learn from the source material?

PRIMARY SOURCES

There are two types of sources: primary and secondary. **Primary sources** are firsthand accounts or direct evidence of an event. Primary sources can be things that are written down, images you can see, or recordings you can hear.

Written primary sources can be personal writings:
■ Letters: Correspondence on paper between people
■ Diaries and journals: Stories written down about daily life
■ Blogs: Journals posted on the Internet
■ Social media: Updates on social sites online

They can also be public documents:
■ Court transcripts: Written account of what is said in court
■ Reports: Documents for businesses
■ Advertisements: Flyers or space in a newspaper, magazine, or website to offer something for sale or rent
■ Lyrics: The words of a song
■ Newspapers: Papers reporting on daily events in a certain area
■ Posters, banners, and leaflets

In the fight for LGBTQ rights, there is a lot of primary written evidence. Old newspaper articles describe the raid by police officers on Mother Clap's **molly house** in London in 1726. Old court documents also describe the trials and punishments for those arrested on charges of homosexuality. These documents give insight into the laws that homosexuals had to live under and the often-deadly results of the beliefs of that time.

▲ At the UN General Assembly in 1949, Eleanor Roosevelt— former First Lady of the United States—holds a copy of the United Nations' Universal Declaration of Human Rights. It has now been translated into more than 500 different languages.

"Sadly, its urgency was illustrated on Tuesday evening outside Howard Theatre when three assailants [attackers] held and stabbed a 16-year-old boy while using anti-gay epithets [hurtful names]. We thank the police for their prompt investigation and arrest of the three suspects, whom we hope to see successfully prosecuted for their hate crime; and we are eager to hear of the boy's full recovery."

Rick Rosendall, then-vice-president for Political Affairs of the Gay and Lesbian Activists Alliance, giving evidence on a hate crime in Washington, DC, June 29, 2012

ACADEMIC SOURCES

University and college libraries also have a lot of written primary sources on the struggle for LGBTQ rights. Both on campus and online, their collections contain meeting notes and newsletters of groups studying or fighting for equal rights. There are also online libraries that hold articles and ebooks relating to the fight for LGBTQ rights.

► Writer and activist Liz Carpenter wrote this letter supporting the Equal Rights Amendment in the United States. The amendment, which sought to guarantee equal rights regardless of sex, was used by the LGBTQ community in later legal battles.

ANALYZE THIS

What information can be learned from personal writings—such as Liz Carpenter's letter—that is not part of official or business documents? Is it important to read both types of primary written source material? Why or why not?

Liz Carpenter

4701 Woodway Lane, N.W. Washington, D.C. 20016

September 23, 1971

Dear Congressman,

As you know, through the years women have been stepped upon, wept upon and slept upon. Still we find something in men to love -- and I will be glad to say this again to every one of you after the Equal Rights Amendment is passed without crippling amendments.

As you know, this issue has been with us since 1920, when women were given the vote. It would have passed by now except for being fogged up by the phony issue of "protective" legislation for women.

It is high time men recognized that some "protective" laws treat women like idiots, and others keep women out of jobs where they'd lift no more than a three-year-old child does.

Don't be fooled by the bugaboos raised by the Amendment's opponents. Women will gladly trade protective laws for some equal pay and equal rights.

I hope very much that you will give this your real support. I have traveled 100,000 miles this past year, and one thing is clear -- women are ready for it, the country is ready for it. Won't you be with it?

Sincerely,

Liz Carpenter

Area Code 202
363-4417
537-1616

P.S. We need your help, Mr. Congressman.

OTHER PRIMARY SOURCES

Visual and **auditory** primary source material can give us a new perspective on an event, a person, or an **era**. Photographs can capture accurate details as they happen. Paintings can show us what the world was like before cameras were invented. Auditory primary sources can be recordings of interviews, speeches, and even music. When we listen to interviews, we begin to recognize people as individuals and relate to their struggles. These ways of presenting information help us gain a better understanding of what we are researching.

Visual primary sources include:
- Prehistoric wall paintings
- Illuminated, or decorated, manuscripts
- Stained glass windows
- Paintings: Images made on canvas with paint
- Posters: Printed images with or without words usually displayed on walls
- Photographs: Images made with a camera
- Movies/videos: Moving images recorded by a camera

▼ Transgender actress Laverne Cox speaks during a news conference at the United States Capitol, Washington, D.C. Cox called for federal surveys to include data on sexual orientation and gender identity.

ARTIFACTS AS EVIDENCE

Artifacts are source material that can give invaluable insights into the LGBTQ story. They include scripts from movies with gay themes, personal possessions of openly gay celebrities, gay bar menus, matchbooks, flyers, and T-shirts. They are a mix of primary and secondary historical evidence (see pages 14–15).

- Maps: Diagrams of a region or area
- Billboards: Large outdoor boards showing advertisements
- Flyers/brochures: Small pamphlets with information about services or products

When we look into the fight for LGBTQ rights, visual and auditory materials are some of the strongest evidence we have. Images of marches and pride parades show **protesters** of every color, gender, and background. Posters and signs from protests and photographs from clashes with police and demonstrators really help us see the fight on a personal level. Interviews with LGBTQ people let us hear the emotion in someone's voice as they describe their fears, worries, or triumphs. Listening to a speech given by gay **activists** can bring us into the moment. Music can sometimes better explain feelings than words can.

EVIDENCE RECORD CARD

Singer Elton John, in concert
LEVEL Primary source
MATERIAL Color photograph
CREATOR Photographer Ian West
LOCATION Madejski Stadium, England
DATE May 26, 2005
SOURCE PA Images

◀ Singer Sir Elton John founded the Elton John **AIDS** Foundation in 1992. (See page 36.)

SECONDARY SOURCES

Evidence that is created after an event or uses primary sources is called **secondary source** material. It is one step further away from direct evidence. It can still be a valuable resource as it is often an interpretation of facts and can shed light on different viewpoints.

It can sometimes be difficult to determine whether something is a primary or secondary source. Researchers often ask themselves these questions when assessing source material:

- Does the author or creator get their information from someone else's work, instead of personal experience?
- Is the creator interpreting events or drawing conclusions, instead of giving facts?
- Is the date of the work long after the date of the event, instead of matching closely with the event?

The following are secondary sources:
- Novels: Stories that might be based on actual events
- Encyclopedias: A set of books or online pages that give a little information on different subjects
- Textbooks: Study books used in schools
- Magazines: Publications that have articles written on a variety of topics
- Histories: Books about a certain period in the past
- TV documentaries: Often a mix of interviews and video material

"To top it off, he was a good brother. He was always there when Snake needed him. Until yesterday, Snake had wanted to be exactly like him."

Snake by Susin Nielsen (2006)

PERSPECTIVES

The book *Beyond Magenta* is about transgender teens. How does the cover portray transgender teens? What symbolism does the publisher use to draw readers in? Is it effective? Why or why not? The book won an award from the LGBTQ organization Stonewall (see page 24).

▼ **Author Susan Kuklin interviewed six transgender teens to craft essays that told their stories from their own point of view.**

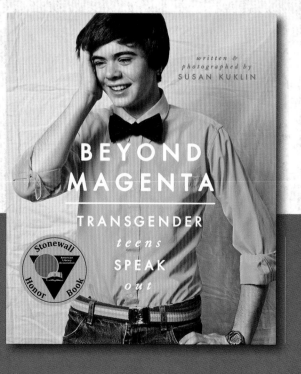

As the struggle for equality for LGBTQ people has really become an issue in modern times, there have been many articles written on the topic. Magazine articles usually use interviews and written primary sources to put forward a particular point of view. Novels such as *Shine* by Lauren Myracle and *Snake* by Susin Nielsen help build **empathy** and understanding of what it is like to struggle for basic rights that others take for granted. Movies are another secondary source of information. *Brokeback Mountain* helped to change the public's views on homosexuals and the damage caused by **homophobia**.

◄ *If I Was Your Girl* author Meredith Russo is transgender herself. The story is partly inspired by her own experiences.

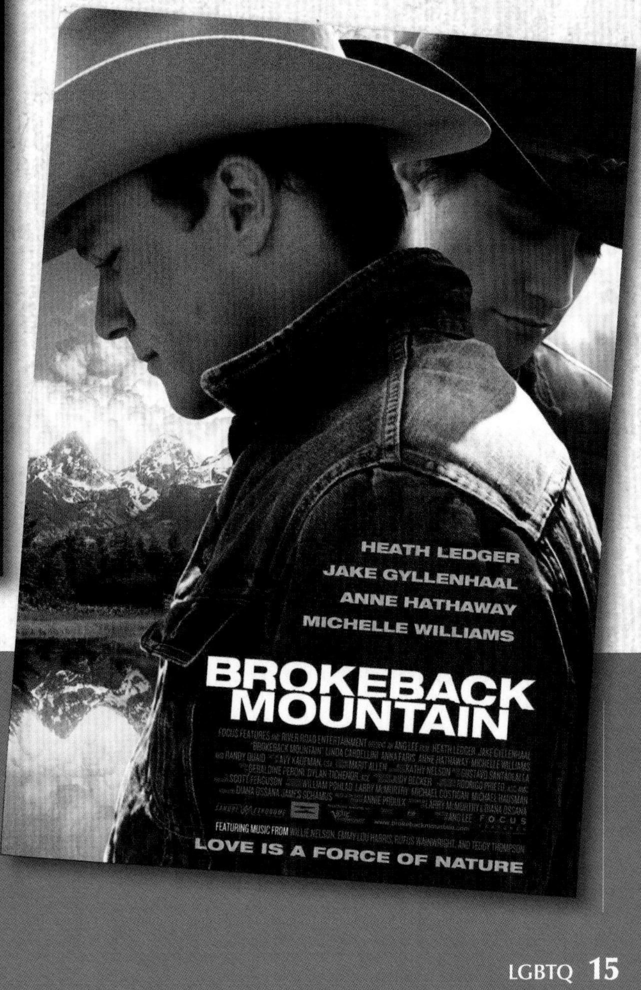

"DEEPLY, ELECTRICALLY INSPIRING."
—Jennifer Niven, *New York Times* bestselling author of *All the Bright Places*

IF I WAS YOUR GIRL

MEREDITH RUSSO

HEATH LEDGER
JAKE GYLLENHAAL
ANNE HATHAWAY
MICHELLE WILLIAMS

BROKEBACK MOUNTAIN

LOVE IS A FORCE OF NATURE

▶ While the movie *Brokeback Mountain* won a Golden Globe and had eight Oscar nominations—and was a box office success—some countries banned its release because of the topic of homosexuality.

INTERPRETATION

"It is our interpretation of the past, our limiting beliefs, and our undigested pain that stop us from being able to move forward with clear direction."

Debbie Ford, U.S. self-help author and lecturer, 1955–2013

Finding source material is only the first step for historians. The next step is determining if the material is accurate and unbiased. **Bias** is prejudice in favor of or against a thing, person, or group. Bias changes how we look at things and how we report on things. If someone thinks a certain type of dog is aggressive, then they will look for signs of that behavior. They will take pictures of that dog attacking or growling. They will report on the number of dog bites from that breed. This can give a slanted picture of the truth about dog breeds. It is the same with historic events or people. If the person writing the report or taking a picture already has an idea in mind about what they are researching, they may change what information they collect or what image they capture.

Historians deal with this by thinking about the **Bias Rule** when looking at both primary and secondary sources. The Bias Rule states:

- Every piece of material must be looked at **critically**.
- The creator's point of view must be considered.
- Each piece should be compared with other sources.

The evidence for the fight for LGBTQ rights might contain a lot of bias because there are very divided views on homosexuality. Homophobia is the dislike and prejudice against homosexual people. Someone with homophobic views might give a very different report of a protest march, parade, or court battle.

▲ The Radical Lesbians group believed in political change from a system run by mainly **heterosexual** men.

PERSPECTIVES

This black-and-white photograph shows a protest march by the group Radical Lesbians. Does the lack of color change the portrayal of the march? Do you think the photographer is showing bias? Explain your answer.

TIME, PLACE, CONTEXT

Bias isn't the only factor that historians look for in source material. They know that the closer the creation of the source is to the time and place of the event, the more likely it is to be accurate. People can forget or change details as time goes by mainly because information or stories can be exaggerated or mixed up as they are told and retold.

Historians use the **Time and Place Rule** to help them determine how accurate the information may be, while

▼ Anti-gay rallies are often organized by religious groups, who refer to religious texts to support hatred and discrimination toward LGBTQ people.

still keeping bias in mind. For example, most reliable to less reliable are:

- Direct traces of an event, for example, a burned-out building
- Material created at the time the event happened such as live TV coverage
- Reports created after an event by firsthand witnesses or participants
- Books created after an event by people who use primary sources

Historians also need to be aware of **context**. Context is the setting in which an event occurs. This can color how we see an event or a person. Ideas and beliefs change over time. What was considered normal and acceptable 200

IAN-BRONX
ON TWO

SUNDAY NEWS

NEW YORK'S PICTURE NEWSPAPER

Largest circ

MANHATTA

New York, N.Y. 10017, Sunday, July 6, 1969

Homo Nest Raided, Queen Bees Are Stinging Mad

By JERRY LISKER

▲ This newspaper from 1969 hangs on the wall near the front entrance at the Stonewall Inn in New York City (see page 24). The Stonewall is a bar where some of the first LGBTQ rights riots happened that year. President Obama later designated the bar as a National Monument.

years ago is not the same as what we believe today. Seeing injustice, violence, and fear can make people challenge old beliefs and come to new realizations. The fight for LGBTQ rights is still pushing against old **superstitions, irrational** fears, and misinformation.

Until recently, homosexuality was seen as **immoral** and made illegal. Newspaper reports of arrests, trials, and punishment for homosexuals were written with the slant that justice was being done. Reports today will be written within the context of a time when there is more acceptance. Researchers and readers need to keep the context of the changing views of society in mind when they look at source material.

PERSPECTIVES

Look at the newspaper headline above. The writer used a phrase referring to "nests and queen bees." To whom or what does this refer? Do the terms show bias? If you saw a headline like this, would you expect the article to be objective and sensitive to the event?

"They searched our van and found a small amount of gay literature. We were informed that we were not to be allowed to enter the United States because the border guard suspected we were homosexuals."

Gay activist Sibyl Frei, writing in *The Empty Closet* gay newspaper, 1978

FIGHT FOR LGBTQ RIGHTS

"It takes no compromise to give people their rights.... It takes no money to respect the individual. It takes no political deal to give people freedom."

Harvey Milk, gay-rights activist

North America was mainly settled by Europeans. Their ideas and customs were brought over with the settlers. This included prejudice and **discrimination** against homosexuality. In Europe, early documents of laws show that homosexuality was punishable by death, often by burning. LGBTQ people were targeted when out in the community, so they gathered in pubs, taverns, or even private rooms in houses to have a safe place to socialize. In England, these places were often referred to as molly houses. When a molly house was discovered, there was constant harassment and raids. Margaret Clap ran a molly house outside of London, England. In 1726, it was raided and 40 men arrested. The trials exposed the fear and hatred of homosexuals.

In the late 1800s, when Canada became a country, homosexuality was officially illegal. It was punishable by death. Documents seem to show that while no one was actually condemned to death, people lost their positions in government and status in society. In 1869, the death penalty for homosexuality was **abolished** in Canada. Homosexual behavior was still considered a crime, however. In the United States, homosexual behavior was also a **capital offense** until the late 1800s. Anyone found guilty was put to death.

▶ This LGBTQ community commemorates the 46th anniversary of the world's first gay march (1970). The march—in New York City—was the largest Gay Pride March in the United States that year.

FIGHTING BACK

In 1948, Dr. Alfred Kinsey published a report that would change people's ideas about human sexuality. It was called *Sexual Behavior in the Human Male*. He later published *Sexual Behavior in the Human Female* (1953). These reports showed that homosexuality was more common than was previously thought. It helped people understand that a lot of what they feared was just normal behavior.

As these reports were being published, the Senate of the United States published its own report. It was called "Employment of Homosexuals and other Sex **Perverts** in Government." This report was very damaging. It claimed that homosexuals, both male and female, would not make good employees. There was a strong bias against homosexuals in this document. It did not use scientific data but instead relied on interviews with other people with the same bias. It concluded with ways to discriminate against gays and lesbians from getting jobs with the government or the military.

▶ Many people thought Dr. Kinsey's work was controversial. This political cartoon shows him running from his work, which is about to explode.

As the government and mainstream society continued to deny LGBTQ people their rights, they fought back by creating the first gay-rights organizations. The Society for Human Rights was founded in 1924. Its newsletter, *Friendship and Freedom*, was the first gay-interest publication in the United States. The Daughters of Bilitis (DOB) was the first lesbian civil and political rights organization. DOB was formed in San Francisco in 1955 and educated women about their rights and supported them when they were afraid to **come out**.

In Vancouver, Canada, the Association of Social Knowledge (ASK) put out its own newsletter in 1964. Its main goal was to educate people and also push to change the laws. It wanted to help the public understand and accept LGBTQ people as normal human beings.

▲ *The Ladder* was the first national lesbian publication in the United States. It encouraged women to "take off their masks."

◄ During the 1960s, Dick Leitsch was president of the Mattachine Society, a campaigning group set up to protect and improve the rights of gay men. He was the gay journalist who reported on the Stonewall Riots (see pages 24–25).

"The means of print production gradually came into people's hands, so it was possible for our little group of lesbians to buy . . . a mimeograph machine for two or three hundred dollars and be in business. As soon as we could learn how to use it, we could be publishers and that's what happened."

Judy Grahn, feminist and lesbian supporter, 1983

ACTIVIST GROUPS DEVELOP

In the late 1950s, there were few places where people could be openly gay or where trans or gender-fluid people could **cross-dress** without harassment. Private businesses and gay, lesbian, and trans establishments were often raided and shut down. Los Angeles's gay and trans hangout, Cooper's Donuts, was raided by police in 1959. The raid caused a riot. It is considered the first queer uprising in the United States. In San Francisco, many transgender people gathered at one of the Compton's Cafeteria locations because they were not welcome at gay bars. At the time, cross-dressing was illegal. The staff at the cafeteria tried to get rid of trans people by calling the police to have them removed.

One night in 1966, the trans customers at the cafeteria fought back against the police harassment and began rioting. The exact date isn't known because mainstream newspapers didn't cover the event. Dishes and furniture were thrown and a glass window was shattered. The next night, more transgender people,

▶ The Stonewall Inn in New York City was where the gay liberation movement gained ground in June 1969.

as well as other members of the LGBTQ community, picketed the cafeteria. The riots were acts of resistance that forced the police and the community to see trans people as humans with rights. Trans people also got together to create their own network of medical and social services with the National **Transsexual** Counseling Unit.

The Stonewall Inn riot happened only a few years later. The Stonewall was a

"He had seen no evidence whatsoever that any form of violence is planned by the GAA (Gay Activists Alliance) for the convention. He expressed the opinion that any form of violence would be in direct conflict with the very nature of most homosexuals, who are peaceful by nature and avoid violence."

From a Federal Bureau of Investigation (FBI) file on a gay activist, March 22, 1972

gay bar in New York City. Like other gay bars, it was raided by the police about once a month. On June 28, 1969, police raided. Many patrons were ushered outside before being arrested and a crowd gathered. A trans woman being arrested yelled, "Why don't you guys do something?" and the crowd rioted.

Even people who hadn't been at the inn that night were moved by what had happened. There were meetings and events to protest against the police action. Stonewall was seen as the birthplace of the gay rights movement. Within two years, there were gay rights groups in every state, as well as in Canada, Western Europe, and Australia.

▶ The Equal Rights Amendment to the U.S. Constitution sought to guarantee equal rights under the law regardless of a person's sex. While many states adopted the resolution in the 1970s, not enough did for it to be passed as an amendment. It has been reintroduced in every session of Congress since 1982.

H. J. Res. 208

Ninety-second Congress of the United States of America

AT THE SECOND SESSION

Begun and held at the City of Washington on Tuesday, the eighteenth day of January,
one thousand nine hundred and seventy-two

Joint Resolution

Proposing an amendment to the Constitution of the United States relative to
equal rights for men and women.

Resolved by the Senate and House of Representatives of the United States of America in Congress assembled (two-thirds of each House concurring therein), That the following article is proposed as an amendment to the Constitution of the United States, which shall be valid to all intents and purposes as part of the Constitution when ratified by the legislatures of three-fourths of the several States within seven years from the date of its submission by the Congress:

"ARTICLE —

"SECTION 1. Equality of rights under the law shall not be denied or abridged by the United States or by any State on account of sex.
"SEC. 2. The Congress shall have the power to enforce, by appropriate legislation, the provisions of this article.
"SEC. 3. This amendment shall take effect two years after the date of ratification."

Carl Albert
Speaker of the House of Representatives.

Vice President of the United States and
President of the Senate pro Tempore

EVIDENCE RECORD CARD

Amendment to the U.S. Constitution
LEVEL Primary source
MATERIAL Government document
LOCATION Washington, D.C.
DATE January 18, 1972
SOURCE National Archives

HARVEY MILK

LGBTQ protests and riots were effective in bringing attention to the issues of civil and human rights, but they did not succeed in creating laws that would help the LGBTQ community fight battles such as workplace or housing discrimination. What was needed was someone in power to change things. Harvey Milk was that person. It was publicly known that he was homosexual and he met with a lot of **opposition**. He was unsuccessful three times in running for San Francisco city supervisor, but he was still focused on pushing for equal rights. After he lost his bid in 1976, he co-founded the San Francisco Gay Democratic Club.

Milk was finally successful in gaining political office in 1977. Although he was determined to help secure rights for the gay community, he was also concerned with all the people he represented. He worked to create day-care spaces for working moms and also build low-cost housing.

▼ Gay rights protesters march during the National Democratic Convention in New York City in 1976.

PERSPECTIVES

Look closely at this image of a gay rights protest march in New York City. What do you notice about how the protesters are dressed, their ages, and what they have with them? What does this say about the diversity of people gay rights affected at the time?

"The only thing they have to look forward to is hope. And you have to give them hope. Hope for a better world, hope for a better tomorrow, hope for a better place to come to if the pressures at home are too great. Hope that all will be all right. Without hope, not only gays, but the blacks, the seniors, the handicapped, the 'us'es, the 'us'es will give up."

Excerpt from "The Hope Speech," 1978. Harvey Milk

At that time, California state senator John Briggs tried to pass a bill that would have gay teachers fired from public schools. Harvey Milk joined with others to defeat this initiative. In one of his powerful speeches, Milk said, "Gay people, we will not win our rights by staying quietly in our closets. . . . We are coming out to fight the lies, the myths, the distortions. We are coming out to tell the truths about gays, for I am tired of the **conspiracy** of silence, so I'm going to talk about it. And I want you to talk about it. You must come out."

On November 27, 1978, former city supervisor Dan White snuck into City Hall and **assassinated** Harvey Milk and Mayor George Moscone. Harvey Milk had received many death threats while in office and had prepared a will with this in mind. In it he wrote: "If a bullet should enter my brain, let that bullet destroy every closet door." Across the country, men and women honored him.

CITY AND COUNTY OF SAN FRANCISCO

Telephone: 558-2145

COMMITTEES:
Chairperson:
  URBAN AND
  CONSUMER AFFAIRS
Vice Chairperson:
  STREETS AND
  TRANSPORTATION
Member:
  COMMUNITY SERVICES

District 5

BOARD OF SUPERVISORS

CITY HALL, SAN FRANCISCO 94102

SUPERVISOR HARVEY MILK

June 28, 1978

President Jimmy Carter
The White House
Washington, D.C. 20500

Dear President Carter:

There has been considerable press coverage of the speech I delivered at San Francisco's large Gay Freedom Day Celebration this past weekend.

In it, I called upon you to take a leadership role in defending the rights of gay people. As the President of a nation which includes 15-20 million lesbians and gay men, your leadership is vital and necessary.

I have enclosed a copy of my remarks for you to read. Especially note the section beginning on page six.

On the November, 1978, California ballot will be an initiative, called the Briggs Initiative, which would prohibit gay persons from teaching and would have other serious infringements on individual rights. Though it is a state ballot issue, it is also of great national importance and we hope you will strongly oppose it.

I would very much appreciate a response to our call for your support and I would be honored to work with you to protect the human rights of all Americans.

Warmly,

Harvey Milk

Harvey Milk

▲ A letter from Harvey Milk to the U.S. president of the time, Jimmy Carter, to ask for his support in rejecting a bill to prevent gay teachers working in schools.

▶ Harvey Milk celebrates his election as a San Francisco supervisor on election night, November 8, 1977.

GRADUAL CHANGE

In the 1970s, the LGBTQ community was becoming more visible and politically active. In North America, politicians were declaring their homosexuality, LGBTQ radio stations and TV shows were hitting the airwaves, and new support groups, such as the Lesbian Organization of Toronto, were being formed. But American and Canadian laws were slow to change.

On October 22, 1977, two gay bars in Montreal—the Truxx Bar and Le Mystique—were raided and 146 people were arrested. The next day, about 2,000 people protested the raids. That led to government action when queer activists demanded changes. In December, Quebec's National Assembly revised the Quebec Human Rights Charter. Discriminating based on sexual orientation became illegal. The Canadian Human Rights Act also came into effect that year. It guaranteed equal treatment for all individuals without regard to many different **factors,** including sexual orientation. Two years later in 1979, Montreal and Vancouver became the first two Canadian cities to host pride marches.

Raids and arrests in February 1981 in a gay bathhouse in Toronto led to protests

▲ Gender selections on new **HIV** and **STD** medical testing forms—and on many insurance applications—now include transgender as an option.

> *"It was about making it easier for people on a personal level; the group gave us permission to explore and express ourselves, and not face the future with fear. We felt and became empowered to combat stereotypes and misinformation about being gay."*
>
> R. J. Alcalá of the Gay Liberation Front in a University of Rochester newsletter, 2010

est You Need?

we'll help you.

Transgender

on the corner of Yonge Street and Wellesley Street. People said the police had crossed a line. In March, a Gay Freedom Rally was held. It is considered Toronto's first Gay Pride Parade.

Barriers were being broken down in sports as well. Renée Richards was born Richard Raskind, but **transitioned** to a woman in 1975. An eye surgeon who was also a successful tennis player, Richards met roadblocks when she tried to play in the U.S. Women's Open Tennis Championships. Richards sued the United States Tennis Association for gender discrimination and won. She paved the way for other trans athletes to compete on the world stage.

ANALYZE THIS

Sports is one of the few areas in which men and women still compete separately. What prejudices did Renée Richards put to rest by winning the right to compete as a female?

◀ Transgender U.S. tennis player Renée Richards fought for the right to play women's tennis. She took her fight all the way to the Supreme Court and won.

MILITARY RULES

LGBTQ people have always served in the military but they had to hide their sexuality or gender identities. The U.S. and Canadian armed services were slow in allowing them to be openly LGBTQ and serve their countries. In 1967, the Canadian military passed an order that allowed it to investigate anyone suspected of being homosexual. Those identified were released from service.

This continued until 1992, when the order was **repealed** thanks to Michelle Douglas. She was a member of the armed forces from 1985 until 1989, when she was released for being a lesbian even though she had a clean record. She sued the Department of National Defense in 1990. Before her trial was over, the military changed its policy on banning gays and lesbians and settled the lawsuit.

▼ These items, including records, buttons, pictures, and signs are being donated to the Velvet Foundation. This foundation is looking to raise money, buy artifacts, and find a place to build a gay rights museum in Washington, D.C.

"Sexual orientation remains a personal and private matter. Sexual orientation and lawful homosexual conduct (statements, acts or same-sex marriage) are not a basis for separation, reassignment or special consideration. Soldiers may inform others of their sexual orientation at their own discretion. The Army will not ask Soldiers to identify their sexual orientation. The Army will not collect or maintain data on an individual's sexual orientation."

An excerpt from the act repealing the "Don't Ask, Don't Tell" policy

In the United States, an order was passed in 1949 banning lesbians, gays, and transgender people from serving in the military. Several homosexual personnel fought their dismissals. In 1993, a new policy was created. It was called "Don't Ask, Don't Tell" (DADT). The military decided that gay, lesbian, and bisexual people could serve as long as they weren't open about their sexuality. After several court challenges, the DADT policy was repealed in 2010.

Matthew Shepard was a 21-year-old gay university student who was beaten, tortured, and left to die in Wyoming in 1998. Two young men were arrested for the crime. Investigators questioned whether Matthew's sexual orientation was the reason for the attack. While lawyers argued this wasn't the case, the media attention on the trial made the public demand new laws around hate crimes. In 2009, the Matthew Shepard Act finally passed. It included crimes based on gender, sexual orientation, gender identity, and **disabilities** as hate crimes.

In many ways, transgender people were **marginalized** in these discussions and struggles. The media and public focused on gays and lesbians. It took until the early 2000s for transgender people to gain recognition as equals and not just allies in the LGBTQ community. Outside the community, transgender people are still fighting for equality rights under the law. This includes the rights to full gender expression and use of the public bathroom of their gender.

▲ On December 22, 2010, President Obama signed the Repeal Act of the "Don't Ask, Don't Tell" policy into law. It allowed LGBTQ people to serve openly in the U.S. Army.

THE ONGOING STORY

"All I can say is from the long view, 50 years, we have moved ahead in a way that would have been absolutely unimaginable back then."

Frank Kameny, gay rights activist, 2011

One of the most visible and well-known aspects of LGBTQ community is the pride parade. Pride parades began as a remembrance and recognition of the harassment and prejudice LGBTQ people endure. In the United States, the first parades took place in 1970 in Chicago, Los Angeles, San Francisco, and New York City, one year after the Stonewall Riots.

In Canada, Montreal and Vancouver held the first pride marches in 1979. The Toronto Pride Parade evolved out of the protest marches that happened after the Bathhouse Raids in 1981. Today, Toronto Pride is a 10-day event that includes a **dyke** march, a trans march, and the pride parade.

The parades and marches are a way for the LGBTQ community to celebrate its diversity and challenge the **stigma** placed on being LGBTQ. Sometimes they are also a demonstration for rights such as same-sex marriage. Pride parades usually include floats, **drag queens**, dance routines, and music. There are representatives of various groups, churches, and politicians. They have spread around the world. In some countries, LGBTQ culture is celebrated. In others, such as Croatia and Bulgaria, it has led to conflict.

Some members of the LGBTQ community criticize the parades. They say they sometimes focus too much on sex and shock value, and not enough on political statements and human and civil rights. Others complain they are becoming too commercial and ignoring the problems still facing the LGBTQ community.

▲ Toronto Pride is a 10-day event held each year in Toronto, Ontario. In 2014, Toronto hosted the fourth international World Pride. Ontario Premier Kathleen Wynne, the first openly gay head of government in Canada, Prime Minister Justin Trudeau (center), and Toronto Mayor John Tory took part in the march in 2016.

PERSPECTIVES

Members of three levels of Canadian government, including the prime minister of Canada, Justin Trudeau, are marching here in the Toronto Gay Pride Parade. What message does their involvement send to society?

THE RIGHT TO MARRY

Legal same-sex marriage has been one of the central rights fought for by the LGBTQ community. The roots for this run deep. As well as wanting to be able to marry someone they love and make a commitment to them, married couples enjoy many other rights. Among these rights are automatic **inheritance**, hospital visitations, parental adoption rights, tax and medical benefits, medical decisions, and retirement plans.

For both Canada and the United States, the fight has mostly been made in the courts. In a challenge in the Canadian Federal Court of Appeal called *Halpern v. Canada*, the marriages of two gay couples in 2001 that were deemed illegal were **debated**. The court agreed that denying same-sex marriages violated the Canadian Charter of Rights and Freedoms and ruled that the two

▼ René Leboeuf and Michael Hendricks were the first gay couple to be legally married in Quebec. Many newspapers and magazines covered the event.

couples' marriages were legal. On July 20, 2005, the government brought in the Civil Marriage Act, redefining marriage to include same-sex couples.

The first gay wedding took place in the United States in 1969. However, it was not recognized as legal and a court challenge failed. In 1993, several gay couples sued the state of Hawaii when they were denied a marriage license. Again, they were defeated. In 1996, President Clinton signed the Defense of Marriage Act. In it, same-sex marriages were not recognized.

▲ A lesbian couple celebrates their marriage at a pop-up chapel in Central Park in New York City.

This setback sparked LGBTQ people to start challenging the law, state by state. Vermont approved gay marriages as civil unions, while Massachusetts was the first state to legalize gay marriage. One by one, states began to change their laws. History was made on June 27, 2015, when the U.S. Supreme Court ruled that same-sex marriages were a legal right across the United States.

"Marriage is a fundamental human right that must not be denied to anyone. Further, no one's rights should ever be subject to the will of the majority. This is at odds with our republican form of government."

Phil Mendelson, gay activist, 2012

THE AIDS CRISIS

One of the most devastating health crises in the United States and Canada has been the AIDS/HIV **epidemic**. DNA studies have shown the disease started in monkeys in the Democratic Republic of the Congo in Africa. Scientists believe it made the leap to humans through diseased monkey meat. It quickly spread and by 1980, was found in five continents, including North America. By the end of 1981, 270 cases of a severe **immune deficiency** linked the disease to homosexuals. This, of course, was not the case, but the idea persisted. It was even called a "gay-related immune deficiency." Some people believed it was an act of God against homosexuals. This idea only increased the problem of homophobia.

Within two years, the number of infected people rose to more than 3,000, with almost 1,300 of them dying. Women and children were affected, as well as **hemophiliacs** and heroin users. In 1984, the cause was found to be a virus referred to as HIV that was spread by contact with body fluids that include blood and semen. Work was done to find a cure. Celebrities such as basketball legend Magic Johnson who announced they had AIDS/HIV, helped to end the idea that it was just a "gay disease" or something to be ashamed about.

▲ The public's fear of contracting AIDS increased fear and prejudice against the LGBTQ community. Posters such as this one were made to help educate people on how AIDS was—and was not—spread.

"Because of its mysterious nature, and I submit, because of the groups associated with it, AIDS has generated something just short of a public panic. A good deal of that panic has been fostered by homophobes bent on turning a public health crisis into an opportunity to attack the gay and lesbian community."

Virginia Apuzzo of the National Gay Task Force, testifying in front of a Congressional committee, 1983

The gay community came together in this tragic time to become more active in fighting for effective treatment. Publications such as *The Empty Closet* gay newspaper printed facts, not myths, about the causes of AIDS and its method of spreading. There were also educational posters to spread awareness and advice. In other countries around the world, including many in Africa, there is denial that HIV even leads to AIDS.

PERSPECTIVES

Look at this image of the AIDS Memorial Quilt. What impact would a memorial of this size have on the people viewing it? By being placed at the center of the nation's capital, what message did this convey to U.S. society and the whole world about the AIDS epidemic?

▼ Started in 1987, the AIDS memorial quilt was 1 mile (1.6 km) long by 1996. Each of the 37,440 panels represents a person in the United States, who died from AIDS.

EVIDENCE RECORD CARD

The AIDS Memorial Quilt
LEVEL Primary source
MATERIAL Textile
LOCATION Washington Mall, Washington, D.C.
DATE October 11, 1996
SOURCE Alamy photo library

THE LGBTQ STORY TODAY

"I think the view we take here is that there's no place for the state in the bedrooms of the nation. I think that what's done in private between adults doesn't concern the Criminal Code."

Pierre Trudeau, Canadian Justice Minister, 1967

In many countries around the world, the rights of LGBTQ are accepted. Societies believe that everyone deserves to be treated as a valued and respected human being. Backward thinking and **unfounded** beliefs and fears are being fought with facts and information.

LGBTQ rights in Canada are some of the most advanced in the world. Transgender people can legally change their names and government documents are **phasing out** or adding other options for a question about gender. Same-sex marriages and adoption for these couples is legal. There are laws in place to stop discrimination based on sexual orientation for jobs, housing, or education.

In Europe, the top five countries in terms of LGBTQ rights are Malta, Belgium, the United Kingdom, Portugal, and Norway. There is a big range in rights across Europe, though. The European Union Agency for Fundamental Rights is an organization that is working to improve opportunities and safety for all LGBTQ people, especially among public officials, healthcare workers, and law enforcement.

However, for all the advances there have been around the globe in the fight to secure equal rights, there are still many places where LGBTQ people are not safe and face prejudice, hatred, and violence.

▶ Unlike many other gay pride parades that began as demonstrations for gay rights, Amsterdam Pride in the Netherlands began in 1996 as a festival to celebrate diversity.

Take a look at this pride parade in Toronto, Canada. Look at the marchers and the spectators. Are there people from different ethnic groups and professional organizations? What does this tell you about who is represented and the level of acceptance of LGBTQ people?

AN INTERNATIONAL PICTURE

Several countries in Africa have some of the harshest anti-gay laws. In Uganda, homosexuality can land you in prison for 14 years. It is common for police to abuse LGBTQ people. Even people who simply mention homosexuality in a play can be arrested and **deported**.

In the Middle East, LGBTQ people have virtually no rights and no protection. Transgender women in Turkey are likely to be arrested and beaten while in **custody**. The murder of homosexuals is at an all-time high. LGBTQ websites and organizations are routinely shut down by the police and government.

Russia is known for its anti-gay laws and deep homophobia. LGBTQ youth have been attacked and beaten. There is no protection from the government or law enforcement against discrimination or hate crimes. Public opinion in Russia seems to be strongly anti-LGBTQ and same-sex marriage is still illegal. Violence against LGBTQ people is on the rise. New laws passed in 2013 ban any written material referring to LGBTQ culture or rights. Pride parades have also been banned and even flying a rainbow flag can get citizens arrested.

Even when progress has been made, a change in government can reverse those changes. In the United States, the new government elected in 2016 has stated that it is prepared to reverse many of the new orders that protected the rights of the LGBTQ community. It has vowed to make same-sex marriage illegal again, as well as ending protection for transgender and homosexual people. Without people from all parts of society making a stand, there is a chance that the rights of people in the LGBTQ community will be eroded.

"Being LGBT does not make you less human. And that is why gay rights are human rights and human rights are gay rights."
Hillary Clinton, U.S. Secretary of State, 2011

ANALYZE THIS

Think of the countries where gay rights are under attack or non-existent. What are basic human rights like in these same countries? Is there a link between fewer human rights and lack of LGBTQ rights? If so, what is the link?

▲ The Women's March on January 21, 2017, was a worldwide protest. Women demanded change to policies around women's rights, immigration reform, healthcare, and LGBTQ rights.

▶ Athletes have been out in sports for many years. Soccer player Robbie Rogers is one of the first openly gay male athletes in any of the major North American sports leagues.

TIMELINE

1726 Mother Clap's molly house in London, England, is raided; three men are later executed

1794 Prussia (now in Germany) gets rid of the death penalty for homosexuality

1832 Russia makes homosexual acts punishable by up to five years' exile in Siberia

1836 James Pratt and John Smith are hanged in the last execution for homosexuality in England

1861 England changes the death sentence for homosexuality to 10 years in prison

1889 Homosexuality is legalized in Italy

1895 Irish playwright, novelist, and poet Oscar Wilde is charged for indecent acts

1897 The first homosexual rights group in England is organized by George Ives

1903 Police in New York City raid a bathhouse and arrest 12 men

1910 Emma Goldman begins speaking publicly for homosexual rights

1924 Henry Gerber founds the Society for Human Rights

1933 German Nazi party bans homosexual groups and sends homosexuals to concentration camps

1937 The pink triangle is used to denote gay men in Nazi concentration camps

1948 Dr. Alfred Kinsey publishes *Sexual Behavior in the Human Male*

1950 Sweden founds the Organization for Sexual Equality

1955 The Daughters of Bilitis is founded in San Francisco by four lesbian couples

1964 Canada's first gay organization ASK, and first gay magazines *ASK Newsletter* and *Gay*, are founded

1965 Compton's Cafeteria riots, in which transgender people fight back against discrimination

1966 The first lesbian showing her face appears on the cover of *The Ladder* magazine

1967 Canadian Justice Minister Pierre Trudeau states that there is "no place for the state in the bedrooms of the nation"

1720

1900

1967

1968

1969 First gay wedding in the United States; it is not recognized as legal

1971 George Klippert, the last man jailed for homosexuality in Canada, is released from prison

1976 Renée Richards is denied entry into the U.S. Open Women's Tennis Championships; she sues the U.S. Tennis Association in 1977, and wins

1977 Harvey Milk is elected city-county supervisor in San Francisco

1978 Harvey Milk is assassinated

1981 The Bathhouse Raids take place in Toronto, Ontario; the resulting protest march is seen as the first Toronto Pride Parade

1990

1992 End of ban on gay people in the military in Canada

1998 Matthew Shepard is beaten to death for being gay

2009 Matthew Shepard Act addressing hate crimes is passed

2013 Kathleen Wynne elected first openly LGBTQ premier of a Canadian province in Ontario

1969 Stonewall Inn riots take place in New York City

1970 The first LGBT Pride Parade is held in New York City

1974 Kathy Kozachenko, the first openly lesbian woman elected to a state legislature, is elected to political office in Ann Arbor, Michigan, United States

1977 Two gay bars in Montreal are raided, leading to protests; queer activists demand changes and Quebec alters its Human Rights Charter

1980 AIDS is found around the world and spreads quickly

1990 Homosexuality is no longer considered an illness by the World Health Organization

1993 "Don't Ask, Don't Tell" policy enacted by the U.S. military

2005 Same-sex marriages legal across Canada

2010 President Obama repeals the "Don't Ask, Don't Tell" policy

2015 Same-sex marriage law passed and came into effect in the United States

2017

BIBLIOGRAPHY

QUOTATIONS

p.4: United Nations online: www.un.org/en/universal-declaration-human-rights

p.8: Hitchens, Christopher. *"Mommie Dearest,"* Slate, October 20, 2003.

p.16: Ford, Debbie. *The 21-Day Consciousness Cleanse.* New York: Harper Collins, 2010.

p. 20: Goldman, Jeremy. *26 Quotes to Help Celebrate LGBT Pride Month.* www.inc.com/jeremy-goldman/26-quotes-to-help-celebrate-lgbt-pride-month.html

p.32: Zongker, Brett. "Gay Rights Papers Shown at US Library." *San Diego Tribune,* May 9, 2011.

p.38: Pierre Trudeau quote: CBC television archives, December 21, 1967.

EXCERPTS

p.6: Goldman, Emma. "Offener Brief an den Herausgeber der Jahrbücher über Louise Michel," with a preface by Magnus Hirschfeld, 1923.

p.10: "Testimony on Hate Crimes in the District of Columbia and Police Response to Reports of Hate Crimes Delivered before the Committee on the Judiciary," June 29, 2012: www.glaa.org/archive/2012/rosendallhatecrimes0629.pdf

p.14: Nielsen, Susin. *Degrassi Junior High: Snake.* Toronto: Lorimer, 2006.

p.19: Jim Monk from an interview with activist Sibyl Frei. *The Empty Closet.* Issue 89. December 1978.

p.23: Donnelly, Nisa. "Selections from Interviews with Judy Grahn": www.english.illinois.edu/maps/poets/g_l/grahn/intexcerpts.htm

p.24: United States Government. FBI memorandum re: Gay Activist Alliance: https://vault.fbi.gov/gay-activist-alliance-part-01-of-02/gay-activist-alliance-part-01-of-02

p.26: Milk, Harvey. Transcript of "The Hope Speech." Museum of Fine Arts, Boston, online: www.mfa.org/exhibitions/amalia-pica/transcript-harvey-milks-the-hope-speech

p.28: Alcalá, R. J. "University of Rochester's Pride Network Celebrates 40 Years." Online newsletter, September 15, 2010: www.rochester.edu/news/show.php?id=3682

p.30: "Support Plan for Implementation." U.S. Department of Defense. Collingdale, Pennsylvania: DIANE Publishing, 2010.

p.35: Mendelson, Phil. Gay and Lesbian Activists Alliance 2012 questionnaire for D.C. council candidates: www.glaa.org/archive/2012/cqmendelson.pdf

p.36: Apuzzo, Virginia. Statement, National Gay Task Force, 1983: http://historymatters.gmu.edu/d/6893/

p.40: Clinton, Hillary. Speech on International Human Rights Day, Geneva, Switzerland, 2011.

TO FIND OUT MORE

Non-fiction:

Belge, Kathy, and Marke Bieschke.. *Queer: The Ultimate LGBT Guide for Teens.* San Francisco: Zest Books, 2011.

Dawson, Juno. *This Book is Gay.* Naperville: Sourcebooks Fire, 2015.

Kuklin, Susan. *Beyond Magenta: Transgender Teens Speak Out.* Somerville: Candlewick Press, 2014.

Polen, Jerome. *Gay & Lesbian History for Kids: The Century-Long Struggle for LGBT Rights*, with 21 Activities (For Kids series) Chicago: Chicago Review Press, 2015.

Fiction:

Konigsberg, Bill. *Openly Straight.* New York: Arthur A. Levine Books, 2015.

Lam, Laura. *Shadowplay: Micah Grey, Book 2.* Nottingham, U.K.: Strange Chemistry, 2014.

Schrag, Ariel. *Adam.* New York: Houghton Mifflin Harcourt, 2014.

INTERNET GUIDELINES

Finding good source material on the Internet can sometimes be a challenge. When analyzing how reliable the information is, consider these points:

- Who is the author of the page? Is it an expert in the field or a person who experienced the event?
- Is the site well known and up to date? A page that has not been updated for several years probably has out-of-date information.
- Can you verify the facts with another site? Always double-check information.

- Have you checked all possible sites? Don't just look on the first page a search engine provides. Remember to try government sites and research papers.
- Have you recorded website addresses and names? Keep this data so you can backtrack and verify the information you want to use.

WEBSITES

The "It Gets Better Project" wants to communicate to lesbian, gay, bisexual, and transgender youth around the world that rights for LGBTQ people get better:
www.itgetsbetter.org/pages/about-it-gets-better-project/

The American Civil Liberties Union has blogs, videos, and other features for LGBTQ youth:
www.aclu.org/issues/lgbt-rights/lgbt-youth

Teen Ink is an online magazine written by and for teens:
www.teenink.com/opinion/social_issues_civics/article/249524/Gay-Rights/

GLOSSARY

abolished Put to an end

abuse The improper use of something

activists People who campaign to bring about political or social change

AIDS Acquired Immune Deficiency Syndrome

amnesty To pardon, allow, forgive, or grant

archives Places that store historical information about a location, a person, or an event

artifacts Objects made by humans, usually with cultural or historical significance

assassinated Murdered in a surprise attack

auditory Related to the sense of hearing

bias Not being completely fair or objective; favoring one thing over another

Bias Rule A guideline for writing history that says historians should think about each piece of evidence critically

bisexual Sexually attracted to both men and women

body cast Shape of body formed by pouring plaster in voids in ground

capital offense A crime so serious that death is considered a punishment

come out To publicly announce one's sexual orientation or gender identity

conspiracy A plan by two or more people to do something illegal or harmful

context The circumstances or setting in which an event happens

critically Looked at to find the good points and bad points and eliminate bias

cross-dress To wear clothing typical of the opposite sex

custody Imprisonment

debated Argued both sides of a topic

deported Sent back to the country where they originally came from

disability A physical or mental condition that limits a person's movements, senses, or activities

discrimination Unjust treatment of someone, especially because of their race, age, or sex

drag queen A man who dresses up in flamboyant women's clothing

dyke A slang term for lesbian

empathy Ability to understand the feelings of others

epidemic Outbreak of a disease spreading quickly

equality The state of being equal, in status, rights, and opportunities

era A long period in history

factors Qualities or facts

fluid In relation to sexuality, a sexuality that is not defined and is easily changed

gay Someone who is sexually attracted to individuals of the same sex, especially men who are attracted to men

gender The state of being male or female

gender fluid A gender identity that changes over time and is a mix of male and female

hemophiliacs People with a disorder in which blood does not clot properly and they can bleed to death

heterosexual Attracted to people of the opposite sex

HIV Human Immunodeficiency Virus

homophobia Dislike or prejudice against homosexual people

homosexuality Sexually attracted to people of the same sex

immigrants People coming to live in a country from another country, legally or illegally

immoral Against principles society follows

immune deficiency Body's immune system has difficulty fighting infections

inheritance Money or property received when someone dies

irrational Not making sense, highly unusual, or strange

lesbian A woman who is sexually attracted to other women

marginalized Treat people as unimportant

molly house Meeting place for homosexuals

opposition People against something

perverts People whose sexual behavior is thought to be not normal

phasing out Slowly getting rid of

prejudice Negative opinions not based on fact

primary source A firsthand memory, account, document, or artifact from the past that serves as a historical record about what happened at a particular time

protesters People who demonstrate against something

queer Broad terms for homosexuals, bisexuals, and transgender people

repealed Taken back

secondary source A historian's or an artist's interpretation of a primary source

sexual orientation Referring to which gender someone is attracted to

sexually fluid people Individuals who experience changes in their sexual orientation over time

source material Original document or other piece of evidence

spectrum A range of differences

STD Sexually Transmitted Disease

stigma Disgrace felt by people

superstitions Incorrect beliefs

Time and Place Rule A rule used by historians to assess how true and accurate a source may be

transgender or trans Person whose gender does not match their birth sex

transitioned Changed from one gender identity to another

transsexual or trans Person who feels that they belong to the opposite sex

unfounded Having no basis in fact

INDEX